ROCKFORD PUBLIC LIBRARY
3 1112 020083289

D1284158

WHAT WE STAND FOR

STAND UP FOR YOURSELF

the kids' book of COURAGE

ANDERS HANSON

CONSULTING EDITOR, DIANE CRAIG, M.A./READING SPECIALIST

Super Sandcastle

An Imprint of Abdo Publishing

visit us at www.abdopublishing.com

Published by Abdo Publishing, a division of ABDO, PO Box 398166, Minneapolis, Minnesota 55439.

Printed in the United States of America, North Mankato, Minnesota
062014
092014

Editor: Liz Salzmann
Content Developer: Nancy Tuminelly
Cover and Interior Design and Production: Anders Hanson, Mighty Media, Inc.
Photo Credits: Shutterstock

Library of Congress Cataloging-in-Publication Data

Hanson, Anders, 1980-
Stand up for yourself : the kids' book of courage / Anders Hanson ; Consulting Editor, Diane Craig, M.A., Reading Specialist.
pages cm. -- (What we stand for)
ISBN 978-1-62403-297-4
1. Courage in children--Juvenile literature. 2. Courage--Juvenile literature. I. Title.
BF723.C694H36 2015
179'.6--dc23
2013041840

Super SandCastle™ books are created by a team of professional educators, reading specialists, and content developers around five essential components—phonemic awareness, phonics, vocabulary, text comprehension, and fluency—to assist young readers as they develop reading skills and strategies and increase their general knowledge. All books are written, reviewed, and leveled for guided reading, early reading intervention, and Accelerated Reader® programs for use in shared, guided, and independent reading and writing activities to support a balanced approach to literacy instruction.

CONTENTS

WHAT IS COURAGE?

Courage is about being brave.

James wears a red cape. He pretends to be a superhero.

Sometimes people must do things they are afraid to do. It takes courage to do these things.

The doctor gives Allison a shot. It hurts a little. But Allison knows it will keep her healthy.

It takes courage to face pain and danger.

Firefighters have courage. They run toward a fire.
Most people would run away.

It takes courage to stand up for what is right. **Especially** when other people think you're wrong.

Martin Luther King Jr. had courage. He stood up for equal rights for all people. Many people disagreed with him.

WHAT CAN YOU DO?

How can you
be courageous?

TRY SOMETHING NEW.

Trying new things takes courage. It can be scary when you don't know what to expect.

At first, Bryan was afraid to try the zip line. Now he loves it!

ASK FOR HELP.

Asking for help takes courage. It's okay to tell someone that you aren't sure how to do something.

Ian asks his teacher how do to a math problem.

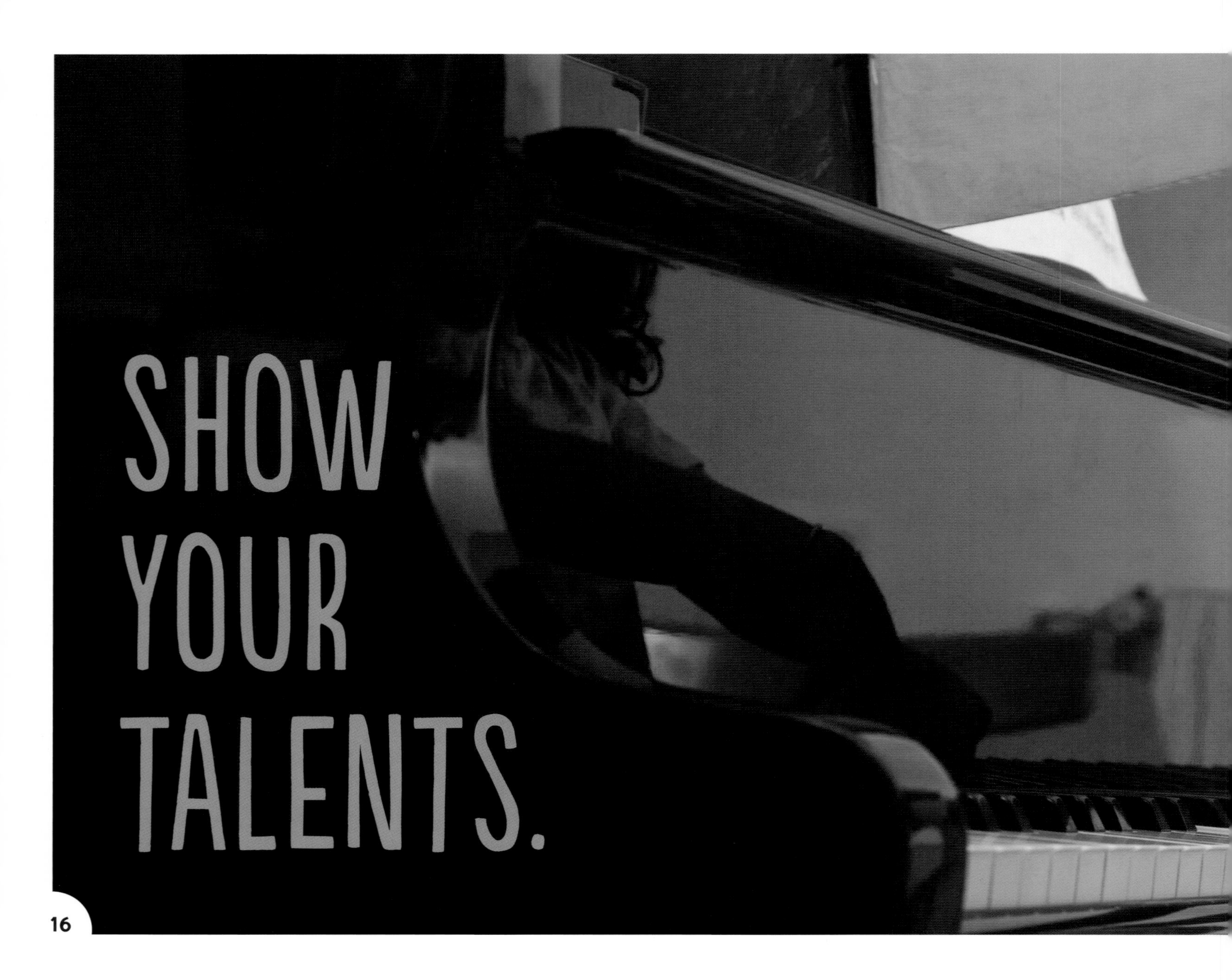
SHOW
YOUR
TALENTS.

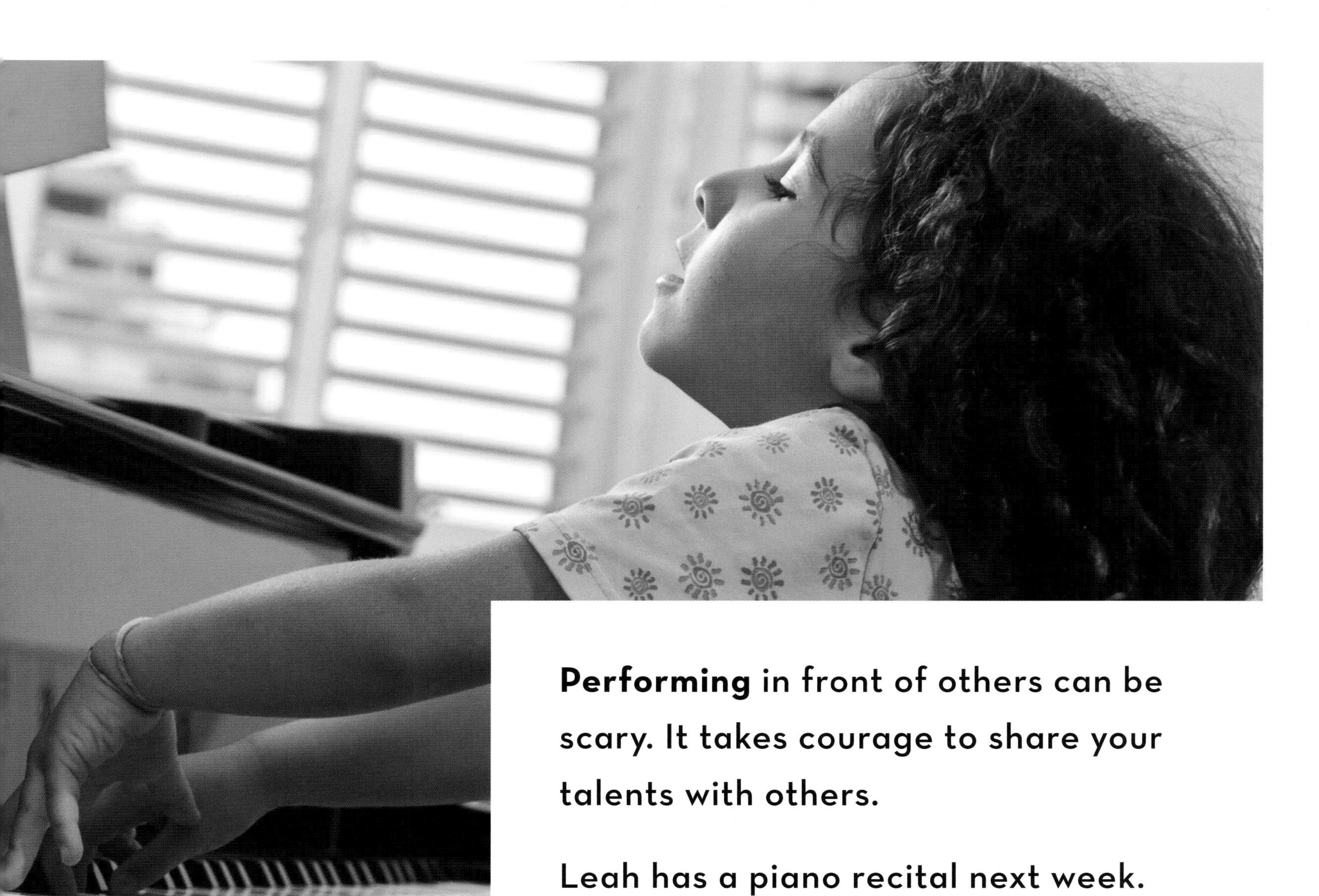

Performing in front of others can be scary. It takes courage to share your talents with others.

Leah has a piano recital next week. She practices the song she will play.

SHARE YOUR FEELINGS.

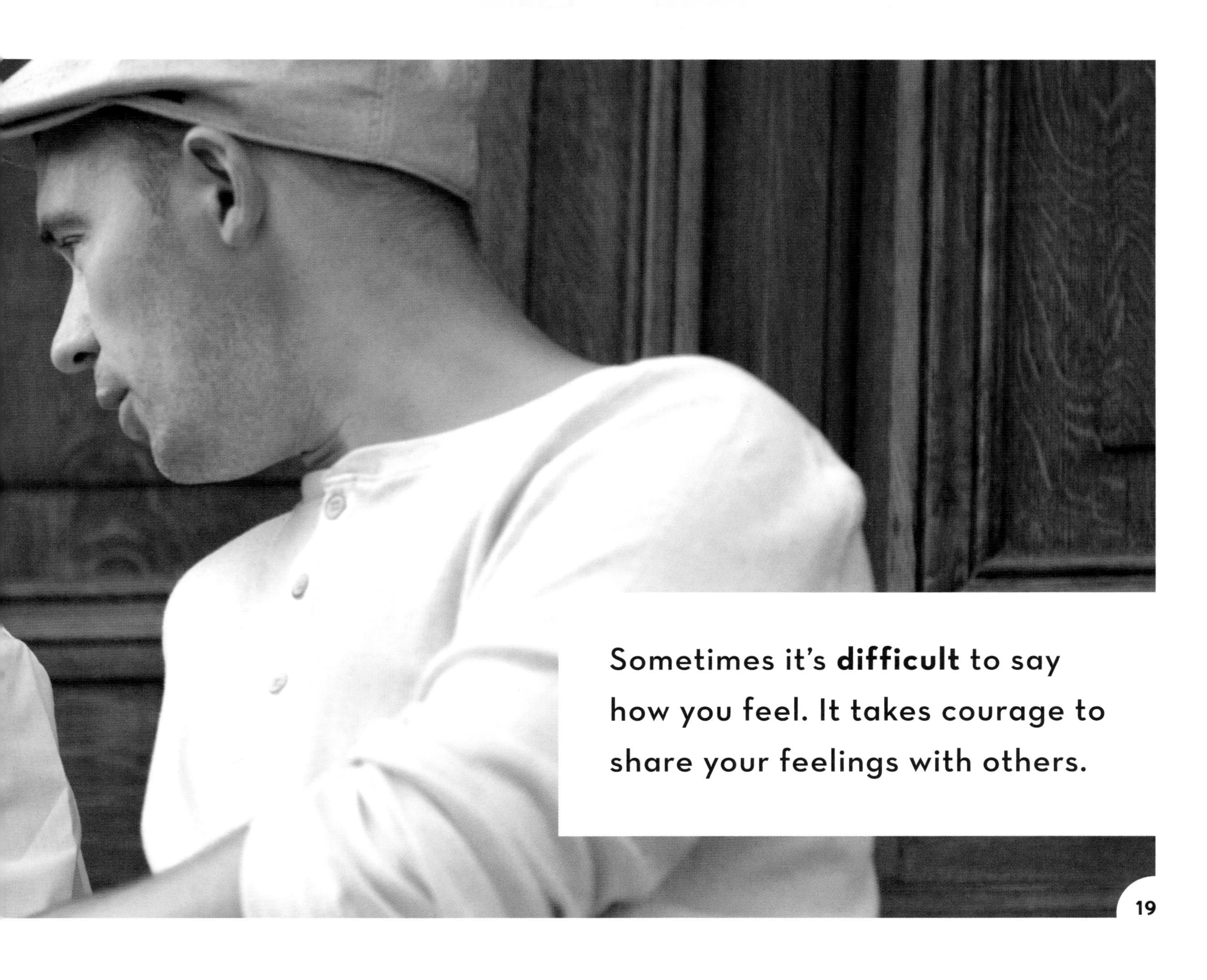

Sometimes it's **difficult** to say how you feel. It takes courage to share your feelings with others.

TELL THE TRUTH.

Sometimes it seems easier to lie than to tell the truth. Telling the truth takes courage.

WHAT WILL YOU DO?

What is one thing you can do to be courageous?

GLOSSARY

DIFFICULT – hard to do, deal with, or understand.

ESPECIALLY – very much, or more than usually.

PERFORM – to do something in front of an audience.